To Elizabeth
from:
Aunt Ann & Uncle Howard "1996"

This edition published in 1993 by Mimosa Books, distributed by Outlet Book Company, Inc., a Random House Company, 40 Engelhard Avenue, Avenel, New Jersey 07001.

2 4 6 8 10 9 7 5 3 1

First published in 1993 by Grisewood & Dempsey Ltd.
Copyright © Grisewood & Dempsey Ltd. 1993

ISBN 1 85698 519 9

Printed and bound in Italy

HUMPTY DUMPTY
AND OTHER NURSERY RHYMES

MIMOSA
·BOOKS·

NEW YORK • AVENEL, NEW JERSEY

ALPHABET PIE

A was an
Apple pie

B
Bit it

C
Cut it

D
Dealt it

E
Eat it

F
Fought for it

G
Got it

H
Had it

I
Inspected it

J
Jumped for it

K
Kept it

L
Longed for it

M Mourned for it

N Nodded at it

O Opened it

P Peeped in it

Q Quartered it

R Ran for it

S Stole it

T Took it

U Upset it

V Viewed it

W Wanted it

XYZ & ampersand
All wished for
a piece in hand

A MAN IN THE WILDERNESS

A man in the wilderness asked of me,
How many strawberries grow in the sea?
I answered him, as I thought good,
As many as red herrings swim in the wood.

BAA, BAA, BLACK SHEEP

Baa, baa, black sheep,
   Have you any wool?
Yes, sir, yes, sir,
   Three bags full;

One for the master,
   And one for the dame,
And one for the little boy
   Who lives down the lane.

THE SKY

Red sky at night,
Shepherd's delight;
Red sky in the morning,
Shepherd's warning.

CORPORAL BULL

Here's Corporal Bull
A strong hearty fellow,
Who not used to fighting
Set up a loud bellow.

THE KILKENNY CATS

There once were two cats of Kilkenny,
Each thought there was one cat too many;
So they fought and they fit,
And they scratched and they bit,
   Till, excepting their nails,
   And the tips of their tails,
Instead of two cats, there weren't any.

THE CUCKOO

Cuckoo, cuckoo, what do you do?
In April I open my bill;
In May I sing all day;
In June I change my tune;
In July I prepare to fly;
In August away I must.

CONTRARY MARY

Mary, Mary, quite contrary,
  How does your garden grow?
With silver bells and cockle shells,
  And pretty maids all in a row.

12

DAVY DUMPLING

Davy Davy Dumpling,
Boil him in the pot;
Sugar him and butter him,
And eat him while he's hot.

13

OLD MOTHER HUBBARD

Old Mother Hubbard
Went to her cupboard,
To fetch her poor dog a bone;
But when she got there
The cupboard was bare
And so the poor dog had none.

She went to the baker's
To buy him some bread;
But when she came back
The poor dog was dead.

She went to the joiner's
   To buy him a coffin;
But when she came back
   The poor dog was laughing.

She took a clean dish
   To get him some tripe;
But when she came back
   He was smoking a pipe.

She went to the fishmonger's
   To buy him some fish;
But when she came back
   He was licking the dish.

She went to the tavern
   For white wine and red;
But when she came back
   The dog stood on his head.

She went to the fruiterer's
   To buy him some fruit;
But when she came back
   He was playing the flute.

She went to the tailor's
   To buy him a coat;
But when she came back
   He was riding a goat.

She went to the hatter's
To buy him a hat;
But when she came back
He was feeding the cat.

She went to the barber's
To buy him a wig;
But when she came back
He was dancing a jig.

She went to the cobbler's
To buy him some shoes;
But when she came back
He was reading the news.

She went to the seamstress
   To buy him some linen;
But when she came back
   The dog was a-spinning.

She went to the hosier's
   To buy him some hose;
But when she came back
   He was dressed in his clothes.

The dame made a curtsey,
   The dog made a bow;
The dame said, "Your servant,"
   The dog said, "Bow-wow."

HUMPTY DUMPTY

Humpty Dumpty sat on a wall,
Humpty Dumpty had a great fall;
  All the King's horses,
  And all the King's men,
Couldn't put Humpty together again.

THREE BLIND MICE

Three blind mice, see how they run!
They all ran after the farmer's wife,
Who cut off their tails with a carving knife,
Did you ever see such a sight in your life,
    As three blind mice?

JACK SPRAT

Jack Sprat could eat no fat,
   His wife could eat no lean,
And so between them both, you see,
   They licked the platter clean.

DOCTOR FOSTER

Doctor Foster went to Gloucester
In a shower of rain;
   He stepped in a puddle,
   Right up to his middle,
And never went there again.

MARY'S LAMB

Mary had a little lamb,
   Its fleece was white as snow;
And everywhere that Mary went
   The lamb was sure to go.

     It followed her to school one day,
        That was against the rule;
     It made the children laugh and play
        To see a lamb at school.
          And so the teacher turned it out,
            But still it lingered near,
          And waited patiently about
            Till Mary did appear.
              Why does the lamb love Mary so?
              The eager children cry;
              Why, Mary loves the lamb, you know,
                The teacher did reply.

TO THE MAGPIE

Magpie, magpie, flutter and flee,
Turn up your tail and good luck come to me.
One for sorrow, two for joy,
Three for a girl, four for a boy,
Five for silver, six for gold,
Seven for a secret ne'er to be told.

PAT-A-CAKE

Pat-a-cake, pat-a-cake, baker's man,
Bake me a cake as fast as you can;
Pat it and prick it, and mark it with B,
Put it in the oven for Baby and me.

GIRLS AND BOYS COME OUT TO PLAY

Girls and boys, come out to play,
The moon doth shine as bright as day.
Leave your supper and leave your sleep
And come with your playfellows into the street.
Come with a whoop and come with a call,
Come with a goodwill or not at all.
Up the ladder and down the wall,
A half-penny loaf will serve us all;
You find milk, and I'll find flour,
And we'll have a pudding in half an hour.

PUSSYCAT MEW

Pussycat mew jumped over a coal,
And in her best petticoat burned a great hole;
Pussycat mew shall have no more milk,
Until her best petticoat's mended with silk.